"Sonlight"

COLLECTION OF POETRY

"Sonlight"

COLLECTION OF POETRY

*Faith—based, simple
poems about everyday life.*

KAREN HUGHES

XULON PRESS

Xulon Press
555 Winderley Pl, Suite 225
Maitland, FL 32751
407.339.4217
www.xulonpress.com

Paperback ISBN-13: 978-1-66289-869-3
Ebook ISBN-13: 978-1-66289-870-9

Preface

Do you know that the word "humor" is not in the Bible? Check the concordance; it is not there. However, "laugh" and "laughter" are there. They are not very frequently compared to other subjects, but they are there.

For example, the word "law," a very serious word, is there seventy times, while "laugh" is only there nine times and "laughter" only four times.

This fact makes me realize that God's Word is more solemn (which is only mentioned two times, by the way) than it is humorous, and that is what He wants us to understand.

"Laughter" is mentioned for sure as well as "joy" (forty-eight times), "joyful" (eighteen times), and "joyous" (two times). So, if you combine "joy," "joyful," "joyous," and "laughter" as well as "laugh," there is a total of eighty-one mentions of these words in the Bible. With that being said, I believe that God does allow us time for joy and laughter.

This small collection of poems came to me on a whim. I am not sure why these words are coming to me now other than the fact that my recent retirement has given me more time to open my mind. You see, I have never written anything in my life except for term papers that were required of me in school.

Summary of Book

In these hectic times in all of our lives, it is nice to be able to have a few moments to just read and reflect on life.

My faith and love for God and Jesus have always gotten me through many difficult times during my life. I believe that these poems have been sent to me from Heaven. It is my hope to be able to share them with you and maybe they will help you as well.

These simple poems are just reflections on life in general, some humorous, some more serious. Hopefully, you will enjoy them as much as I have enjoyed writing them. Perhaps you will find them helpful. If nothing else, you may find some humor in them.

For several days during the winter of 2023, these rhymes just started coming to me during the night. After waking up, I would jot them down and revise them when I had time. Some have a little humor in them, some are a more serious read. Whatever your preference—serious or funny, my hope is that you enjoy them.

So, grab a cup of tea or coffee, find a relaxing and calming place, and read a little book instead of your phone.

You may find it to be a refreshing change and will make you want to make more time for reading books!

May the Lord Jesus fill your lives, hearts, and minds with joy as He has with mine!

Table Of Contents

Our Hearts. 1

Memories. 5

Angels 7

Boys and Girls 9

Our Future. 11

Kindness 13

Flowers. 15

Seasons. 19

My Poems 25

Listen. 27

Time. 29

Someday 33

Family Tree. 35

Reflections on Marriage 39

Vacation 43

Edward and Bernice 45

Ruth. 49

The Garden 53

Bees 57

Remo and Riley 59

This poem is a reminder to everyone that, no matter how much your heart may be hurting, there is always our Lord and Savior looking out for us.

Our Hearts

Our hearts are like a puzzle.
Many pieces of our lives put together.
Each puzzle piece represents those wonderful moments
and the love we shared together.
They can illustrate our family, friends, and acquaintances too,
even our dearly beloved pets have been a love so true.
Each one is very special to us, and we will always hold
them near,
for even though they may no longer be with us,
their memories to us are oh so dear.

Each person who has touched our lives
has touched our hearts as well.
Our love for them remains with us.
The stories of them we love to tell.

Our hearts store a wonderful reflection
of good times and memories.
It is how it can be broken when those dearly loved ones leave.

They may have simply lost touch with us,
or circumstances caused them to move on,
but in our hearts, they will always be there.
They are never really gone.

So, when your heart is aching,
find comfort in those memories and know
that the love that you shared with your dear ones
will never really go.

Yes, the pieces of your broken heart
are the signs of their love for you.
If you find that you are lonely,
know that God and Jesus are always with you there too.

Yes, cherish those fragments of memories
when you are feeling blue
because it is then that you will come to realize
a love so absolutely true.

When you feel like you can't go on,
Just think of the wonderful times you knew.
You will find some way to pick up those pieces,
put them back together, and start anew.

This will only be accomplished in God's own time for sure.
Because He is the only one who really knows
just how long it will take for a cure.

Your heart will always be yearning
to find love and kindness too.
But always remember, the love and kindness that you have
given away will always come back to you.

> Scripture: 1 Chronicles 28:9: And you my
> son Solomon, acknowledge the God of your
> father and serve him with wholehearted
> devotion and with a willing mind, for the
> Lord searches every heart and understands
> every desire and every thought. If you seek
> Him, He will be found by you; but if you
> forsake Him, He will reject you forever.
> Consider now, for the Lord has chosen you
> to build a house as the sanctuary. Be strong
> and do the work.

Sometimes, when we reflect on our memories,
it becomes easier to face the days ahead.

Memories

When we think about our yesterdays—
of the days that have gone by,
thoughts flow to us like rivers
and sometimes can make us cry.

The times that were beautiful memories
are the ones we like to get.
The memories that were so painful
we simply try to forget.

In our youth, we are so active.
We live, make mistakes, and grow.
It is only in our older years
that we really appreciate those errors so.

For the lessons of life run deeply,
and over time, we can see

that our Lord and Savior was with us back then
to help us learn from these.

So, cherish all those memories,
both the good and not so good ones too.
And remember that no matter where you go
God and His Son Jesus walk along with you.

> Scripture: Psalms 145:7: One generation
> shall praise thy works to another and shall
> declare thy mighty acts.

Have you ever wondered if there really are angels among us? Well, the Bible speaks of them frequently.

Angels

I have sensed the angels many times throughout my days.
They have shown their presence to me in many different ways.
A gentle breeze when the days are just not going quite right.
Or a light tap on the shoulder that wakes me up at night.

It is as if they are saying, *Don't worry or fret.*
We are with you now and please don't forget.
They seem to have sent me these poems,
just some words to live by.
This is certainly startling to me,
and I am really not sure why.

Many loved ones I knew are now gone from this earth.
I am older now and not sure of my own worth.

I love God, Jesus, my country, and family too.
But sometimes when I am alone,
I just cannot think of what to do.

There just seems to be so much trouble throughout some
of my days.
But the angels gently come to me
and try to show the ways.

When alone, I sometimes miss the people
whom I've loved and are now in Heaven.
Can it be that they are the visitors?
That they are those angels sent to me from Heaven?

Yes, I truly believe God sends these angels to me
as a reminder that someday, with them in Heaven,
I will also be.

> Scripture: Psalm 91:11: For he will
> command his angels concerning you to
> guard you in all your ways.

The next two poems sum up what parenting is all about.

Boys and Girls

They come to us from Heaven above,
wee babies, so small and fragile too.
We love, care for, and comfort them
as only parents can do.

We hold them in our hearts and minds
and think of them all our days.
We watch them grow into adults
and never want them to go away.

But their lives are their own lives.
We simply show them the way
to prepare them for their own journey.
God never intended for them to stay.

So, savor every moment watching them play with their toys.
Love and cherish those little girls and boys.

Because one day you will wake up
and they will suddenly be women and men
and the memories of those little ones
will be all you have to think of then.

God's most precious gift to us is our children.
They are very special to Him, you see,
And I thank Him each and every day
for sending these blessings to me.

Oh, sing praises to our Lord above
for these wonderful, generous gifts of love!

> Scripture: Mark 10:13-16: People were
> bringing little children to Jesus for him to
> place his hands on them, but the disciples
> rebuked them. When Jesus saw this, he was
> indignant. He said to them, "Let the little
> children come to me, and do not hinder
> them, for the kingdom of God belongs to
> such as these. Truly I tell you, anyone who
> will not receive the kingdom of God like a
> little child will never enter it."

Our Future

Our children are our future.
They come to us to learn.
They want to know about everything.
So they can grow and take their turn…

To make decisions and sometimes teach *us*
a new and better way.
They leave our nests for better places
but we do long for them to stay.

We love them all so dearly.
Sometimes we forget that they are learning.
We think it is better to do things for them
instead of understanding their yearning…

For a chance to show their skills and knowledge.
Yes, they simply just want us to see.
They are really growing up
and just finding out how to be.

God sent these little lives to us
To help them grow into men and women too
who will understand His gentle ways
to live and work things through.

So, love and teach your children
and remember that, someday very soon,
they will be the ones to change our world
as only they should do.

> Scripture: Psalm 103:17-18: But from everlasting to everlasting the Lord's love is with those who fear him, and his righteousness with their children's children—with those who keep his covenant and remember to obey his precepts.

Kindness

Kindness is such a good thing.
You should show it every day.
So, touch a heart and you may find
some kindness may also come your way.

If you see someone who seems to need a lift,
a kind word will go a long, long way.
You may brighten their lives for only a moment.
But it just might make their day.

I think our Father in Heaven
looks upon us every day
to show His love and tenderness
by allowing us to find nice words to say.

It only takes a minute to smile and show you care.
You may find the time you take to help another
may really make you aware…

That we all need to be reminded
in these busy, hectic times.
That there are people who really need our love and attention.
Yes, a kind word or action really does go a long way.

You may also find that this will also brighten your day!
And I know that God and Jesus really like us
to shine their light and love this way!

> Scripture: Ephesian 4:32: Be kind and
> compassionate to one another, forgiving
> each other just as Christ forgave you.

This next poem reflects some articles recently published in magazines relating to preserving a spot near our homes for wildflowers to grow. They have discovered that not only is it therapeutic for us to enjoy the beauty of flowers, but where they grow also provides an area for wildlife to thrive as well. Hopefully you can find a small area to do this where you live to enjoy the bees, butterflies, and other creatures that will find this area of your home their own. Of course, there is a little correlation in this poem between the flowers and our children as well.

Flowers

Let's not pick the flowers; let's simply let them grow.
The light and love our Savior gives them
is all they need, you know.

Let's not cut the flowers.
Let them grow just where they are, of course.
The stems that our Lord provided to them
are their life sustaining source.

His plan is always different than ours,
if only we could see.
Their beauty calls us to share them, though,
with everyone we meet.

His roots of love run deeply for them,
if only we could know,
but we naturally desire for everyone
to see just how they grow.

Let's not move the flowers.
Let them stay just where they are.
The soil provides their nutrients, and the rain gives
them a drink.
God never really intended them to grow
Anywhere that we should think.

Some lives are like the flowers.
We pluck them from their roots.
We place them in vases for all to admire
so that we can boost.

Alas, if we could only know
His plan is not for us to show,
but rather to feed and nurture them
and simply watch them grow.

His love for us is like this.
He nurtures and lets us grow.
We will never really understand
how deeply this is so.

Oh, He understands our weakness
to want to share them with the crowd.
Who would not want their little buds
to make them oh so proud?

So, let's not pick our flowers.
Just simply let them be.
Then, one day in the future,
His unfailing love, you will truly see.

And it is only natural to not want to let them go.
But His plans are not our own plans
as we all surely know.

Sing praises to our Lord in Heaven for our wonderful,
glorious life.
For giving joy and purpose and very little strife.
Our days, just like the flowers, are limited here on earth.
So, savor every moment.
Never worry about their worth.

No, please do not pick our flowers.
Really let them live!
Only then will you sincerely understand
just how abundantly He alone can really give.

For He gives us our lives as a gift from above
and I know that this is true.
And just like a tiny flower,
He will always love and nurture you.

> Scripture: Song of Solomon 2:11: For lo the
> Winter is past. The rain is over and gone.
> The flowers appear on the earth. The season
> of singing has come, the cooing of doves is
> heard in the land.

This is the first poem that I have ever written. It came to me in the middle of the night during the winter of 2023.

Seasons

It seems it was only yesterday
the fragrance of springtime softly filled the air.
The grass was filled with morning dew.
The days seemed as though they would never end.

Flowers were blooming with brilliant color
and warmth filled our lives from sunrise to sunset.
All of life was fresh and new
just as the dawn awakens a brand-new day.

The sun shone softly in the afternoon sky.
A single, brilliant star to guide us through.
We laughed and played into the evening
until the moon and constellations lit up the sky.

We took the time to observe and ponder
the grandeur and beauty of these stars twinkling in
the darkness.
We could only imagine the vastness and wonder of
our universe.
A divine confirmation of our Creator's power and
gifts of life.

Then, summer arrived with his radiant beam.
We swam and watched the clouds roll by
with no cares, no worries, no thoughts of tomorrow.
Just living life at its peak of ripeness.

Loving each day and tasting the earth's sweet bounty.
Savoring the coolness at night.
A welcome relief from the heat of the sultry daylight.
Facing those mighty storms headstrong.
Never stopping to think how.

Just surviving and thriving through the lightning,
thunder, and rain with awe and wonder.
Fearless and happy.
Grabbing onto each moment of life and never letting go.

Oh, summer!
God's warmest and most joyous season of all.

Soon the winds change,
and autumn arrives with a subtle chill in the air.
There is valid proof of an abundant harvest in the
garden of life,
the earth is changing and so are we.

Oh, how we defy it at first,
holding onto the life we knew as long as we can.

Then all those beautiful colors begin to emerge.
As if God has painted our world overnight with His own
paintbrush.
We savor the sights and sounds,
and the memories of life in a gentler time.

Soon the days become shorter.
It is almost as if we are reading one of those great novels,
nearing the end and never wanting to put it down.

Darkness comes earlier and we long for more light,
but nature says it is not meant to be.
Our Father in Heaven is preparing us for a different
season now.

The air becomes much cooler
and the life that was so warm and beautiful begins to fade
as winter shows his face.

Oh, the beauty of this season, though we think it is not.
The earth takes a well-deserved rest
and our lives do as well.
Barren trees and fields make us sad,
but we only need to remember there is a purpose for all
this calm.

Remember God's words.
Be still and know.
As the snow falls gently on our land,
it is as if He has provided her a warm, comforting blanket
saying *rest, peace, relax, my beautiful child.*
A needed and welcome change is here.

Our own rest and sleep have become easier now.
As the days grow shorter,
Nightfall arrives even earlier than in autumn.

Then a little reminder of His reason for this time of the
Earth's quiet and rest of regeneration and renewal.
Can it really be?

A tiny speck of brightness appears through the
blanket of snow.
A wee crocus bud reaching its leaves to the sun
just as a baby reaches for his parents.
Signs of new life beginning again!

Spring will arrive soon.
The grass will turn green.
And the daylight will stay longer.

Oh, this wonderfully amazing cycle of life.
That only our Maker can provide
forever through eternity…. always.

> Scripture: Acts 14:17: Yet He has not left Himself without testimony: He has shown kindness by giving you rain from heaven and crops in their seasons; He provides you with plenty of food and fills your hearts with joy.

These next few poems are just some funny, whimsical thoughts that came to me from time to time. Hope you like them.

My Poems

My poems can make you happy. Rarely do they make you sad. Some people think they can cheer you up when you are feeling bad.

My husband thinks they are corny
but all I am really trying to do
is help some people get a little laugh
and think of some thoughts that are kind of new.

These words, they just come to me,
and I think they are traveling from Heaven above
to fill my empty times here
with some of God's humor and love.

So, I hope you will enjoy these poems.
Whether on paper or on the screen.
And have a tiny little break.
To relax and simply dream.

Scripture: Psalm 126:2: Our mouths were filled with laughter, our tongues with songs of joy. Then it was said among nations, "The Lord has done great things for them." The Lord has done great things for us, we are filled with joy.

Listen

Listen to your heart.
Not just the beating.
What is it telling you?
Are you doing what it is heeding?

Deep inside our hearts, we all have a yearning.
It is up to us to use our hearts for the learning...
of how our Lord and Savior would like us to live.
Because this life of ours
is what He really gives.

You know in your heart what you want to do.
Now, through Jesus's love,
you will find a way to see it through.

Yes, my prayer for you
is to simply ask God and Jesus what it is He would like
you to do.
Then, through His Holy Spirit,
an abundant life will be given to you.

Scripture: Acts 15:7-9: After much discussion, Peter got up and addressed them: "Brothers, you know that some time ago God made a choice among you that the Gentiles might hear from my lips the message of the gospel and believe. God, who knows the heart, showed that he accepted them by giving the Holy Spirit to them just as he did to us. He did not discriminate between us and them, for He purified their hearts by faith.

Time

Time is of the essence.
What does this really mean?
We can say that time is a collection of minutes,
but is that something that can be seen?

We look at the clock to tell us about the time.
On each hour, certain clocks are known to chime.

Is time just passing, or is it really life?
What if we have no way to tell time.
Would we have so much strife?

It appears we are always rushing
to make more time to do another thing.
But what if we just forgot to keep time
and the chimes were not to ring?

God gave us the sun to rise in the morning.
He gave us the moon and stars to brighten the darkness.
If we would only watch these constellations in the sky,
I wonder if time would simply pass us by.

We would still rise under the sun,
work and play in the light.
And then still sleep in the darkness during the night.
No rushing, no schedules, just learning to be.
And observing in wonder each flower, bird, and tree.

Remembering God, our Maker, and thanking Him each day.
For giving us the life He has provided for us to stay.
So, rejoice in this daily cycle of life and His unfailing love.
And thank Him and worship Him for His gifts from above.

Our lives today would not allow us to have no
schedules for sure!
But we can still find the time each day to thank God for
His gifts so pure.

So, time is of the essence may simply mean
that life is what you make of it.
Instead of rushing about and just getting through
so that you can make everything fit.

Let's take time to appreciate the best of life each day.
If you feel there is not enough time,
simply find a better way.

Then you may see that His love for you is very true.
As you take the time He gives you
to do what He wants you to do.

Scripture: Psalms 104:19-23: He made the moon to mark the seasons, and the sun knows when to go down. You bring darkness, it becomes night, and all the beasts of the forest prowl. The lions roar for their prey and seek their food from God. The sun rises and they steal away; they return and lie down in their dens. Then people go out to their work, to their labor until evening.

Someday

Someday will come
and what will you do?
Are you prepared for what someday can mean for you?

We always say *I'll do that someday,*
But what if someday was today?
Because someday will certainly be here.
Maybe tomorrow or in a day or ten.
When someday arrives, what will you do then?
Will you be ready and able
to lay all those someday promises on the table?

Just give it a try and maybe you will see
that today is just as good as someday will be.

> Scripture: Psalm 121:7-8: The Lord will
> keep you from all harm. He will watch
> over your life; the Lord will watch over
> your coming and going both now and
> forevermore.

Family Tree

When we find out we are going to be parents,
hopefully it is a joyous time, or maybe not.
No matter what your reaction,
the results are going to be a little tot.

You may read up on parenting and take many folks' advice,
but nothing really prepares you
for this new, tiny little life.
You will have those midnight feedings,
and changing of diapers for sure,
but you will love and cherish this little one,
whose life is so fresh and pure.

They are little gifts from Heaven above,
God provides them to us to nurture, protect, and to love.
We teach them to learn His ways,
as they grow up through their days.

There will be times when you wonder
why you were ever given this little blessing.
Like when you think you just cannot possibly
clean up but another of their "messing."

Parenting is indeed a challenge,
but just remember this,
nothing in life compares to a sweet hug, a smile,
or a gentle little kiss.

Little boys will collect some things
like rocks and insects too,
and sometimes will come home from an adventure
with mud all over their shoes.

Little girls will pretend to be princesses,
and enjoy a daily afternoon tea,
with all her little dollies and teddy bears
dressed up in their very finest,
lined up for all to see.

When it is time for them to start to their schools,
it may be difficult for the children
to remember all those new rules.
Just know they will make many new friends
and learn so very much too.

Yes, they will surely learn many new things (both
good and bad)
that they may never have been able to find out from you.

When they become adults and it's time to leave the nest,
it is now time for the parents
to take a well-earned rest.

Of course, you will miss them.
You know we always do.
But the time has now come for YOU
to take care of YOU.

So, escape for a while,
because soon you may hear
that your children's time for parenting
will be very near.

A wee tiny baby will soon be in *their* nest,
and they, as parents, will be longing
for *your* well-deserved time of rest.

Yes, sometimes parenting can be exhausting.
But really, don't you see?
God gives us the work as parents
to build a family tree.

Scripture: Galatians 4:19: My dear children, for whom I am again in the pains of childbirth until Christ is formed in you, how I wish I could be with you and change my tone, because I am perplexed about you!

Esther 9:28: These days should be remembered and observed in every generation by every family, and in every province and in every city. And these days of Purim should never fail to be celebrated by the Jews nor should the memory of these days die out among their descendants.

Reflections on Marriage

When two people decide to marry,
There are so many things to take care of.
They rush about and make those plans
But the main reason for marriage is love.

Love is a very simple word.
Four letters is all it is.
But, oh my, love's definition is so very deep.
Without love, we simply cannot live.

We sometimes say that love is blind,
But can that really be true?
Perhaps it seems that love is nothing
Until it comes to you.

This poem is about marriage,
A sacred union of husband and wife,
A celebration and the beginning of a new harmonious life.
Together each and every day,
Making plans and praying too.
Sharing your days and working things through.

You may have hopes and dreams of children
By starting a family.
If the Lord blesses you this way,
What a wonderful life it can really be.

May God and Jesus travel with you
Along your journey each day.
May you find comfort in Their love for you
In times when things go astray.

Because marriage is not always joyful.
There may be rough patches along the way.
Together you will get through them, though.
If you ask for forgiveness and pray.

When you grow old, as we all do,
And look back on your lives woven together,
May you find abundant blessings beyond all measure
With many wonderful happy memories
To think of and to treasure.

So, when you think of marriage
Try to remember it is not only planning a wedding,
But a life together eternally
To have, to hold, and to cherish.

Yes, marriage is certainly a work of art,
And the finished product is up to you.
With God and Jesus providing the canvas and paints
The result will be honest and true.

>Scripture: Luke 20:34: And Jesus said unto
>them: The children of this world marry and
>are given in marriage.

We all need that time of rejuvenation, relaxation, and rest.
What a better way than on a vacation!

Vacation

We all need a little vacation.
A time to get away.
A place to journey to and relax.
It doesn't matter where you stay.

Perhaps you may choose the mountains,
tall and majestic and steep.
Or maybe you might journey to the river,
where the waters run very deep.

Some people prefer the ocean seashore
to wiggle their toes in the sand.
And watch the strong and mighty waves
come crashing into rocks and sand.

No matter where you chose your vacation,
you have to simply know,
God's words and Holy Spirit will follow you there.
So just hop in the car and go!

When you arrive at your destination,
there are oh so many activities you can do!
But remember God's plan for you
calls for rest and relaxation too!

Now, whether you gaze at the tall mountains
or bathe in the deep blue sea,
His mighty hands created it all for us.
So relax, enjoy, and simply be!

This section of poetry is very personal. It is about members of my family that are very dear to me. Edward and Bernice are my parents who passed away many years ago. Ruth is my dear mother-in-law who passed just this year.

Remo and Riley are our friendly pets. I hope you appreciate these words in reflection of their lives.

Edward and Bernice

There once was a couple
who found they were in love.
They were definitely brought together
with help from above.

Edward was a farmer.
Bernice was a cook.
For whatever reason,
they both took a second look.

They decided to marry
and start a family.

They never realized what a challenge
their lives would really be.
Edward worked hard on the railways you see,
and Bernice made shoes at a factory.

After working all day,
they returned home again to work.
Edward took care of the house and gardens,
and Bernice would clean and cook.

They raised up three children.
I am sure it was not easy.
They discovered life was never intended
to always be breezy.

When their oldest child was just twenty years old,
He didn't come home one night.
He was called back to Heaven.
It was said that his car was a terrible sight.

Their lives were very empty.
It just did not seem fair
that death would take him from them so early in his life.
It was as if God did not care.
But God's plans were His plans for this family.
Nothing could ever make their lives the same you see.

Their oldest daughter got married
and raised a family too.
I am sure it was also very difficult

for her to get through.
So many fond memories of her dearly beloved brother.
There never would be or ever could be another.

Their youngest child came late in life for Edward and Bernice.
She was only ten months old during this awful tragedy.
That little baby was little old me.

While growing up, it was confusing not to ever know
my brother.
It is as if he was not even real.
I only knew of him through my mother.

She told me of his kindness and his gentle loving ways,
and I pray that I will meet him on that very blessed day
when Jesus calls me home to Heaven
to be with my family.
What a glorious day it will surely be.

Edward and Bernice (my parents), my brother, and aunts
and uncles too!
I wonder if I will even know what to do.

Until that day comes,
I will enjoy my days here,
praying that God and Jesus will always hold me near.

Scripture: Colossians 3:20: Children obey your parents in all things: for this is well pleasing unto the Lord.

Proverbs 12:28: In the way of righteousness there is life; and in the pathway there is no death.

Ruth

What can you say about a dear lady named Ruth?
One thing is for certain, she always told the truth.

She lived a quiet, simple life,
loving her children and family.
She taught us tenderly how to live
and just to simply be.

She prayed for us each and every day,
and this I know is true.
Even if she only knew you for a little while,
she would definitely pray for you too.

Her lessons in life were kind ones.
You could always go to Ruth.
If you were blessed to have her in your life,
she would listen with understanding
and never judge you.

She taught that, if you loved the Lord,
He would always be there for you.
He would never let you down.
His unending love was always true.

She was my friend and neighbor.
A dear one in my time of need.
She always had an open door to "sit a while,"
and she also loved to read…

…Her Bible was a worn one
from years and years of praying.
And if you went to visit her
by her side, the book would always be laying.

And when she was not reading "The Good Book,"
you would find her in the kitchen.
Ruth was also a wonderful cook.

She not only served her delicious food,
but she nourished your soul as well,
and shared her many good times stories
with "you all" as well.

Her life was a long one,
ninety-seven- and three-quarter years.
When she passed, it was very hard
for her children to hold back all those tears.

God called her back to Heaven
so she could reunite with Howard (her spouse) and
all her kin,
and there is comfort in always knowing.
she will be waiting there one day
when He calls us all back in.

I am so very thankful for the time she filled my life with joy.
And oh so very grateful that I found a good relationship
and marriage
with her oldest little boy.

God blessed her life with many children.
Her legacy lives on in each of them for sure.
Their love for one another, like hers,
will always be gentle and pure.

Sing praises to our Lord Jesus and God in Heaven
for blessing our lives with Ruth.
May we always remember her life and love
and God's gospel truth!

> Scripture: 1 Timothy 5:2: Treat older
> women as sisters, with absolute purity.

My husband is a gardener! He spends much time working the ground in our garden in attempts to grow things. Some years are a success, some not so much. We do enjoy the bounties the Lord provides, whatever they may be. The garden has been a blessing to us and great therapy.

It gives us something to look forward to in the winter as well as exercise in the other seasons. It gives us something to work together on. He plants and harvests, and I work in the kitchen preserving and cooking our produce. Hopefully, you may find some time to plant a few things and watch them grow (just like God in Heaven does with us).

The Garden

Nothing says life like a garden.
The garden is where we all got our start.

God's first gift of human life was in the garden.
Adam and Eve enjoyed that rich abundance.
Their lives were pure and simple.

All that they needed, God would provide.
There was no need for them to work.
Even though they had no clothes,
they didn't feel that they needed to hide.

He warned them of the danger,
but their weaker side shone through.
And when that serpent tempted Eve,
she chose the wrong thing to do.

Beginning in springtime, we start to work in the garden.
We plow all the soil up.
Then we till the soil
and plant the seeds from a cup.

The sun and rain provide the elements
for the little seeds to grow.
We watch the ground with anticipation.
And hope that we have no more snow.

At last, the ground cracks open,
and we see a little green.
A sprout that starts a new life
will soon be on the scene.

Then the labors begin
to get that seedling to grow.
We need to water and nurture,
just as God does in our lives.

When the tiny plants bud into flowers
the bees will take their pollen to their hives.
God provides the bees
to take care of the pollination
so that all the plants can produce and thrive.

Now there may be some predators.
The bunnies and deer like to eat for sure!
But there are natural ways to deter them
by planting marigolds around your garden and more.

Be it vegetables, be it fruits,
all food starts in a garden.
So, when harvest time arrives,
and you have done your chores,
what a happy time that is to enjoy
those bountiful gifts from heaven.

Yes, all of life begins with a garden,
but in wintertime, it takes a rest
to prepare the soil for the springtime
when the cycle begins again.

So why not start a little garden in springtime?.
It does not have to be very large.
It can provide a means of therapy and spiritual growth.
The "fruits of your labors" will be a blessing as well.
And it can provide many stories for you to also tell.

> Scripture: Genesis 2:8: And the Lord God planted a garden eastward in Eden; and there he put the man whom he had formed.

Bees

Bees are buzzing in the air.
Bees are flying everywhere.
Get too close and OUCH,
they can give you stings.
But the bees are such amazing, tiny little things.

Without them in our gardens,
the flowers and food would not grow,
They are so very meaningful and important
as you may already know.

Their buzzing to us may sound funny,
but they are working their wee wings ridiculously hard
to help make the honey.

You see, they collect the pollen from the flowers
to take back to their hive.
But as they are buzzing and flying around to do their chores,
they also help make all plants thrive.

Hopefully, our world will always be here
as long as there are bees.
But sometimes all that pollen they carry
can certainly make us sneeze!

God gave us bees and flowers and trees
to give us abundant lives.
We should help to take care of the bees
and also protect their hives.

So, when one of those bees comes buzzing around,
please don't think she is a pest.
Instead, just enjoy watching her work,
as you take a little rest.

The next poem is kind of like the dessert in this collection of poetry. It is about our dearly beloved Shelties (Shetland Sheepdogs). With them in our lives, we never have too much time to be sad.

Remo and Riley

Remo and Riley are my closest friends.
Faithful and loving until each day ends.

Yes, they are with me all day
and I like it that way.

They follow me around
and are always full of fun.
They brighten up my days
as they run and play in the sun.

They play in the yard,
they play in the house.
It's only when they are sleeping
that they are quiet as a mouse.

Remo likes to speak loudly
if someone strange is about.
Riley has a really silly habit.
He just wants to always chase a rabbit!

They listen to my troubles
and about my happy times too.
Never do they tire of
finding things to do.

They provide a simple reminder
when it is almost time to eat
and both enjoy telling us
when they would like a little treat.

Our lives without them are difficult to imagine.
You see, we got them as pups from an Amish farm
and the breeder seemed to think, if we adopted both,
there would really be no harm.

They are brothers, you see,
sent from Heaven above.
He sent them to us at the time we were ready
to cherish them and to love.

Remo and Riley are our pet Shelties,
and if you knew them you would know
how they sometimes are silly
and like to put on a show.

Our Lord God gives us the animals
as these companions and friends
to help us enjoy our lives here on earth
until one day it ends.

This is the conclusion of my *Sonlight Collection of Poems*.
Hopefully you have found a few moments of relaxation
as you read them. Please consider trying some of the
suggestions in the book, maybe a small area for solitude
in a wildflower patch, or a few vegetables or fruits in
a small garden or containers.

And be sure to love and cherish your children, our greatest
gifts for sure! Make some wonderful memories with them
to cherish when you are older. Also, make time in your
lives for the people who came before you (our elders)
because you can learn so much from their experiences.

Whatever you chose, I hope and pray God will bless you
abundantly in your lives as He has in mine.

Godspeed!

Acknowledgements

To my parents, Edward and Bernice, for giving me a firm foundation and for teaching me to love reading in my youth.

To all of the families that have been a part of my life for their care and support throughout all the years.

To my son Jason, his wife, Molly, and his daughters Hannah and Zoe, who have added joy and purpose to my life.

To my daughter Julie and her husband, Todd, as well as their daughters Megan, Jazzmin, Harmony and Melody for allowing me to be like family with them.

To my dear friend Mary Sue Martin for raising my beautiful granddaughters and helping me keep the faith all these years.

To my husband, Harl, for believing in me even when my ideas sounded completely crazy.

To my sister Donna for being my rock of family and faith.

To God for blessing me with an abundant life and for sending these words to me to share.

To Jesus for giving His life on the cross so that we ALL may live forever with Him eternally in Heaven.

Author Bio

Karen Hughes grew up and resides in rural South-Central Pennsylvania with her husband. She is retired and blessed with a blended family of six granddaughters and two great-grandsons. She enjoys reading, painting, knitting, crocheting, cooking, and spending time with her husband, children, grandchildren, and her two Shetland Sheepdogs (shelties), Remo and Riley. *Sonlight Collection of Poems* is her first publication.